# KEYHOLE IN THE SUN

# KEYHOLE IN THE SUN

MATTI SALMINEN

ISBN-13: 9780692965504
ISBN-10: 0692965505
Library of Congress Control Number: 2017915529
CreateSpace Independent Publishing Platform
North Charleston, South Carolina

*In Loving Memory of*
*Carolyn Adams Salminen*

# KEYHOLE IN THE SUN

Imagine a large keyhole right at the center
of the sun; and all light
which emanates on this earth, and gives us life
and warmth, is the imagination of a poet.
Our poet is resting casually under a large
oak drifting off into dreamscapes,
which he creates, and he is our world.

Imagine looking through our sun's keyhole,
and into another universe, and still further;
we could look right into the heart
of the poet whose imagination
is this world's light. I believe
that in looking into his heart
we would see an orchestra tuning their instruments
—as he sleeps. When they played,
and while our poet was awake, their music
would carry over all the cosmos as if time ceased.

We would, upon hearing this music,
stand still at the edge of a bottomless chasm,
and here no thought could exist.
All that was inside us, and which radiated from us,
would be as pure as a small child.
We touch this poet, whose heart plays the music
that causes time to stand still.

# HOW I'VE LOST MYSELF

I'll be frank, and I'll say that it is nice out today. Often,
I look to the outdoors to inspire poetry.
I conflate the darkness of night—or the lightness
of a spring breeze—with the divine nature of being human.
But in this poem, I will note that it is sunny, and I will move on.
All I want is to say, I've lost myself to writing.

# AWAKEN YOUR OCEAN

Sunrises bring about the days
and each one eventually fades;
oceans are the same except theirs are waves.
Stand in the ocean
—even for a second—
and step into the absence of what has been lost,
eternally.
I am no vagrant surfer or penniless mystic.
But, tides and waves and sunrises, all
are a mixture of the very fabric of my soul.
Deep, I am.
But my waters
are in one instant, a drop.

Reside in the soul that breathes as the mountain's winds.
Become the sunrise that beckons the day.
And be lost at every moment
which you've stood in an ocean
because only there will you have been fully awake.

## HAIKU #1

What are stars
in the sky, but my eyes
finding their center

## HAIKU #2

Burn the house
to the ground that the nails
may be retrieved.

## HAIKU #3

The sky is lost
to the light of the
moon and stars.

## ALL OF RIVERS

I've been by the riverside
many many times. I've fished rivers.
I've swam rivers.
I floated on a log with two childhood friends
to an island on a river.
I've listened to rivers.
I've felt I understood rivers.
But all I have
of times spent with rivers—I have because
I left it all behind.

# HEART SONG

Every time I walk this street
I notice a tree I had not, ever before.
Or there will be a person whom I do not know.
And in a small town like this
strange faces can be hard to come by.
Walking this street,
I pass by the cemetery where I once made love;
the same cemetery,
where I once sat in the cold rain, and cried.
It is a strange street with a strangeness
that is close to my heart.
And the closer to my heart I am,
the easier it seems to wander
a little longer, a little further.

## HAIKU #4

The rot of my
loneliness gives to each breath;
mother to child.


## HAIKU #5

All morning the sun
rose—until I forgot myself—
the late afternoon.


## HAIKU #6

What I relinquish
of this world I use to create
my own god.

## AS WE WANDER

I sit and see a friend
walking by with a pile of books in hand.
Curiosity in the multitudes
—in my friend's passing—in what
my eyes grant of the world, rises
and falls. Synchronicity allows
that I wander, and this has always been good,
even when bad.
My friend and I were to have
an apartment together, and now we are not.
My friend's wanderings
must be as good for him as I hope,
are they not? The sound of laughter
interrupts my thinking.

# DREAMS I'VE MISSED

I've imagined myself a woman with whom
you've found love.
I've imagined myself the sunshine
that I get to wake you up.
If I could be your lover—I'd also be your friend.
But you are my wind of winter—my night time mist.
You are the dreams I've reached for
and missed, missed, missed.

# I LOVE POETRY

I tell people that I am reading poetry,
as I look up from my book,
mind slowly re-entering focus
after being lost in verse and they say, poetry
too often, doesn't make sense
that poetry is obtuse...well...
the truth is
that I write poetry
and sift through poem after poem in reading
to be one with other poets
—it is a dream, poetry—
and in loving poetry
we experience abandonment
and we experience the loss of how things must be
as only can be done in dreams,
and with poetry
we become the vessel that speaks,
to that things just are that much more,
and that much more.

## HAIKU #7
A woman ran by—
saying hello—otherwise I
wouldn't have noticed.

## HAIKU #8
I left behind the
illusions of this world and
created my own.

## HAIKU #9
I can't write,
except that I am wind,
words fall as rain.

# HOW MY NOTEBOOK SMILES AT ME

The next page of this notebook is somehow torn;
a leaf turned bright yellow,
and fallen,
but it's not even summer. My mind
flies off with it, into breezes. It does not stop.
It does not look back to see me following.
Falling gently to the ground,
turning leaves tell of frosts,
and of bitter winds shaking them loose of mother trees.
They are nature's smiles,
amidst sweet teardrops falling from skies into puddles.

## HAIKU #10

Clouds hang over
the lake as if god thought, he
was himself, thirsty.

## HAIKU #11

The name I utter
when I pray,
seems that it echoes.

## HAIKU #12

Horizons and their
seas; both are as if braided
with winds and tides.

# LIVE IN RAIN AND BE COLORFUL

All of our kisses, and other pure acts of love,
are reaching down into the earth
as roots into soil, and finding god.
Faith is dutifully returned.
And dutifully, I soak myself
in the raindrops and sunshine
of the heavens. I share my colors—
as if I was the incarnate rose of another lifetime
—and share myself with friends.
Family. Lovers.
But I can't move towards childhood
and become more colorful
as I age. I will wilt and I will die—but
of this beautiful garden, am I.

# GIFT OR DEMON?

Of all my gifts,
if left with only one,
I'd choose to keep my demons;
abandon them now,
and tomorrow there might be other ones.

# IF I CAN'T STOP THE RAIN

Outside rains fall from the sky—
electrified are the greens of grasses.
I have a place
to seek shelter, but
I need to feel the nakedness of being
in the rain. I need to live so that
I may fully appreciate
all that is mine. I need
to live so that I know that
nothing at all is really mine.
I need to have collateral
with which I'll draw from
on rainy days.
Outside, tree branches bow under
the weight of laden leaves.

## HAIKU #13
I've drifted too far
to ever return—the path narrows.


## HAIKU #14
I'm an intra-
stellar traveler who's left
entire worlds behind.


## HAIKU #15
I'm an image of the ever expanding consciousness.


## HAIKU #16
December is too
much, too far, too cold; and spring
will always follow.

## WATERED DOWN

Walks I take between
moments of inspiration.  The times
that connect them; and times
that I am pelted, by raindrops;
winds that have me shivering.  I wonder.
I love and I am lonely.
But will never—ever—but,
sometimes, when I am walking.

# LOVE THAT BURNS

Of the love I have, there is a piece
that I want to give to you.
Of the bond we've forged,
there is something that cannot be ignored.
My words are not as beautiful
as you are. But I will try
to show how deeply I feel your heart.
I want to hold you
and touch your lips.
I want to know you,
and be somebody, you put your trust in.
Hold my hand
and walk by my side,
be with me baby. Together,
we can love and burn brighter
than any star in the sky.

# CRUSHED LEAVES FELL

My heart is crushed
like a leaf fallen,
and left behind until the first snow.
Grasses of late autumn
lie matted against the earth as I do—
in this love sick stupor—holding
to the idea that you too,
want me close. Snows of autumn
wet the roots of trees,
from which crushed leaves fell,
as my pen bleeds love.

## HAIKU #17

The others of
this world transform our
unfolding rhythms.

## HAIKU #18

With the voices
of ghosts, I was released
from the gallows.

## HAIKU #19

It's not how you've
found enlightenment, but if
you've chosen to live.

## HAIKU #20

Here; all things
of motion are converging
as thought.

# NAKED PAGES

I
I love with the love I have, because
deep in the hurts
which I've so painstakingly healed,
I see a reflection of the hurt I cause.
I love with the love I have, because
I want to outdo myself
every time I fall—to risk harder
—and live better.

II
I worship all that is beautiful with the words I have,
because I want to grab hold of something
which allows me to go beyond myself.

I worship all that is truthful with the words I have,
and will continue, until I open a wound
right in my heart.

No lack of words will stop the bleeding;
no thoughts will stand between me and my readers.
Every page that I deface with ink
will bring me directly to spilling forth, revelation.

# LEFT OF THIS WORLD

If I drew a picture there would be black
at the center.  Thoughts would have been lost
in this.  If I sang a song
my words would sound as
the language of mountains; notes
carrying like winds.  Like first snows
of winter.  Like shadows which are
like sleep like my soul; left of this world.

# SHADOWS CAST

In the woods, I am,
yet before me there are no trees.
And no shadows cast
by turning leaves.
Off trail I've wandered.
I have ceased to know a way back.
But with every passing hour
what I carry
becomes light
and less a burden on my back.
Before very long
evening sky will turn to night.
My journey into the forest
will test my spirit,
and my might.
But as journeys go—
not all turns take us
where we want to be.
Getting lost can find us
in places which, otherwise,
we would not know,
nor could we even see.
And this is why there are forests
with no shadows cast
by turning leaves.

# HELD FROM WITHIN

Outside, everything looks brighter…here I am
… I am hidden and remain held within my own grasp
—there is no release—no relent
from my breaking heart; desperate attempts I make
at leaving behind my demons;
without them I would not know who I am—so they follow—
but I keep myself from slipping further;
I feel the necessity of holding pitiful sorrow in high esteem…I am
hidden
…not meaning I am kept apart,
not by a physical,
not by an external—influence—I am my own warden,
holding myself behind my own bars;
I could let go and be free, but I am beset
by latent self-denial, by passions
diluted with apathy…here I am…I am not kept apart
but cannot see any way around—crazy.

# GREEN AND ON THE GROUND

I want to write a poem—
and I want this poem
to contain a leaf.  But how
might I approach this without using
the common inferences
in poems about leaves?   The leaf cannot
be changing color
—and cannot be falling.
However, it may be on the ground.
But it is a green leaf
and may be an aspen for good measure.
The leaf must bear
some significance to the movement
or lyricism
of the composition.
The leaf must exist in the poem
in a manner askance
than which it is in nature.  In nature
the leaf is small and inert;
in the poem it is large,
and exerts influence.  My poem is
about poems, and it has
a green leaf lain on the ground.

# WHAT RESIDES IN THE IDEAS I'VE YET TO HAVE?

I wander. I venture out to uncover
unspoken truths, so that I may—think them
—and write them. And this is poetry.
I'll also heed the instructions of the night.
I'll get up in the middle of darkness
and embrace my inspiration.
I cast off the constraints
which rested on my shoulders while there was light.
I live. And beyond this I must not live,
but I am not afraid. I will have had
at least two or three loves; and otherwise,
I will have answered the call
of blessings which, too often, are left to lie.

# GIVEN TO FAITH

Night falls upon my winged mind
as if I was fallen to blindness. I hasten my step,
but do not outrun the darkness
without misadventures. Outside,
the last moments of winter are
but a memory trying to be reborn. Brisk winds
guide me down side streets,
I discover nothing. I detour in other ways.
Not all races are won by haste,
and emptiness restored, requires a little faith.

## HAIKU #21

With a little
freedom; all things lost become
passion and strength.


## HAIKU #22

I look at the pretty
things; and think. I can't leave
nothing behind.


## HAIKU #23

I've walked over these
stones as though I was blind;
and tasted the dirt.

# PURPLE AND PINK

After a short walk through town, I sat down on green grasses to stretch, meditate, and read. Shade was cast and late summer breezes were cooling. Amidst this reprieve I happened to catch sight of a singular worm. Purple and pink it wriggled as though it was caught in the grasses where I sat. I took notice. And this was pleasing. Curiosity grabbed a hold of my spirit, I reached out, and without comprehension I grabbed the worm and attempted to pull it from the grasses. To satiate my appreciation for this specimen of nature—and see the worm from a closer perspective—I killed.

# FUCK THE ANT COLONY

Today, I have nothing to worry about.
Almost nothing. There is that ant colony
living in the kitchen of my first floor apartment.
But I mean to say that I am free. And by that
I mean that I don't have to work.
Fuck the ant colony, anyway.
Today, I am a poet...an artist of words.
Today, I will live as if living meant something.
Tomorrow, this fantasy will die.
Tomorrow, it will be reborn and it will fade.
But I cannot lose my way, as I am an artist.
If I ever find that I have forgotten how to live,
I will create.

# BIRD OF TRANSCENDENCE

I didn't realize it at the time, but
something small
made a big impression on me.
There was this bird.
It nested nearby a bridge
in a college town, and I loved
to stand and watch it. I believe now,
that that bird was the incarnation
of dreams which have taken root in my soul.
And these dreams
have been cultivated, as if my life
was a gift made to pay homage
to this bird.
I believe that the soul of this bird
and my own
are intertwined.
I believe I will become this bird
or the next step
in this bird's path towards enlightenment
in another lifetime.
And then this bird and I
will experience each other as old friends.

## HAIKU #24

Beyond that post that
lay by the roadside—right there
—nothing else matters.

## HAIKU #25

Listen down into
the pit of your belly and
find nirvana.

## HAIKU #26

The thorns of the rose bush
do all the work.

# IT ESCAPES ME

My eyes see only forward—and in looking back
—I see only myself. All that was
was as it was that I made it my own. And much too much,
I've escaped that which I have been most a part. Truth.
All I've turn towards
to find examples of truth
have lead me to destroy that which it once stood for.
That is I and that is you. That is all we have ever ignored.

# HOW I'VE LOST THE WAY TO YOUR DOOR

I've followed footpaths on a map, but I've lost which way is north.
Yesterday there was a potted flower
which I believe I saw with you before.
But by this potted flower there was nothing more.

Maybe I'm unlucky to be so lost
and not know whether to go or stay some more.
If I stopped could another person come along and tell me where you are?

This map has led me by the water;
I have seen mountains and more;
but no one on my travels has pointed me to your door.

At first I thought my map would bring me to your feet, and the more.
But since all the trails I've wandered—I've wondered
—what ever could this map be for.

In this land which I have thoroughly explored,
I've come to enjoy your mountains;
and I have places in which I've rested—there are three or four.

My map has shown me
being lost is not just a bit of misfortune—there is something more.
Other maps have taught this to many explorers before.

So I'll venture out into the wide open...and maybe...I'll find myself at
your door.

# NAKEDNESS ON ICE

An image of a naked man sliding on ice
—it seems hard for my mind to penetrate.
But this was the image offered
by my horoscope.
And I'm attempting
to welcome this image into my soul;
as such, this poem is an attempt
at manifesting spiritual awareness
from the abstract.
And maybe, a naked man sliding on ice is
symbolic of just such a manifestation…fuckit.
I came to this café to write a poem, anyway.

## HAIKU #27

I hear the bird
sing and am reminded
of my longing.


## HAIKU #28

Go into a forest
and scream; the trees will release
your tired soul.


## HAIKU #29

As a light morning
haze fell over the meadow;
birds were waking.

# SUNSHINE SHIRT

I am a ray of sunshine born onto Harold's shirt.
Warming Harold's world that is my work;
he wears me out so I can shine
and be bright as the day.
Birds sing as I round street corners—
greeting me do they.
But sometimes it gets cold and Harold keeps indoors;
sometimes it rains and sometimes it pours.
I am a ray of sunshine and this is good for me
but others too need to be able, just to be.

# SAY IT, BUT NOT TOO LOUD

Writer's say—say what you mean.
I mean to say,
a little too often, I feel like giving up.
And I don't want to say that in a poem.
Writing gives me strength.
And if I pour through my feelings of sorrow,
and confusion,
maybe that strength will fail.
I write as if I were stronger
than I really am;
but for all of my life I've been alone.
I've tried. I've failed
and I've tried again.   All these years
of solitude have made me…hungrier.  But,
I find myself slightly adrift.

## HAIKU #30

A question crosses
lips as the lonely moon
rises in the sky.

## HAIKU #31

How can a journey, so
long, have brought me to such
a familiar place?

## HAIKU #32

I left myself
to descend from another
galaxy.

# WHY I AM NOT HOMELESS

It was a warm March day,
and I set out to grow myself up, just a little.
I hitch hiked to Montpelier
where I thought I could be homeless.
The roads on my journey
were not quite shaded by trees that still had no leaves.
And the sun peaked through
to help me feel, as if maybe,
I was changing.
I had little more
than the pouch of tobacco in my pocket.
All the more willing I was,
to languish away my comforts,
for a little freedom and independence.

I reached my destination,
but found there was no shelter
in Vermont's capital.  I went a little further—
both in my heart and in my travels.
A man at a church
told me of a shelter in a neighboring town;
I'd fill my belly at a soup kitchen
before the day turned to night,
and that was good.  It was good to feel
as if I had forfeited my naivety,
and was better for it.
It was good to feel
as though I was spreading my wings,
even if slowly.

The next day was fiercely cold.
And I stayed,
in a slightly warm entrance,
to a pharmacy.  And bummed cigarettes
from a lovely young lady,
who was leaving after a day of work.
But because she had seen me on her way in,
she asked if I had been there all day.
I don't remember my reply.
I remember denying that I was homeless.
And I remember giving up
on growing and changing shortly thereafter.

# DISTANCES

Imagine looking off,
over the ocean and past the horizon,
and seeing a small child
on a foreign shore.
But in place of this child
is a lover's quenched thirst to be in love.
And this child—
found on such a distant shore
—is enchanted
by a small shell.
But in place of this shell is a kiss.
What a beautiful thing
is the excitement and joyfulness
of a child
that it is beyond entire oceans
as a precious
and miraculous thing of nature.
Imagine,
losing yourself in the ocean.

## HAIKU #33

Have the cosmos
conspired that I fall
towards freedom.


## HAIKU #34

My heart seems so proud
to get lost and lost. And I
am losing patience.


## HAIKU #35

Waste the times which
you've not been in love. You'll not
regret their passing.

# OF FIRST LOVES

I am a balloon with a slow leak
at the knot of me. My fate is sealed.
I am torn—
and will fall gently to this earth
as I am exhausted. My life
will have been short
but I will have carried
the imagination of a beautiful child.
I will not have perished
without first filling my soul of love.

# STEP TOWARDS FREEDOM

Birds –
they have no need for steps.
And if it pleases you,
you may criticize that point.
Of course birds get around on their feet,
I know this.
This poem is only an attempt at beauty
in written form;
it is a futile step towards freedom.
I am not a bird.
I do not have wings.
As such I have much work to do
and many steps to take.

# SET ME FREE

At work, dreamscapes are like stars
on a cool night with scattered clouds, I escape.
I wish that, as I venture high above these clouds
into the clear and starry sky,
that I could adapt, and learn to fly.
And then I sink back to earth,
remember to stay busy, do my job, and be alert.
But I believe that if I can take one thing
from my dreams and make it real,
I will be cast up into the heavens for good.
This spirit which I embody now,
will be ablaze with the fire that set if free.

# COLORLESS DREAM WORLD

Of all things which I've held close to my heart, I've held closest the weight of broken dreams. And it is broken dreams that have taught me to rely on those who love me. And it is broken dreams that have taught me how to rebuild, and begin over and again. But of all things which I've distanced myself from, I'm most disquieted by the making of these dreams into reality. It is because I fear love more than anything else. It is because I find solace in wisdom and hide among the angels—away from all that our world has to offer. I fill my soul with quiet and knowledge—but I leave my heart to ache. I am left wondering if my image of beautiful is simply as pallid as the moon.

# BE A BEE

If I were to be a bee, I'd want to drink the nectar
Of a daisy, and fly away,
as soon as I had my fill; carrying daisy pollen,
with the winds.  If I were to find love,
I might just have it be fleeting—I'd want to fill myself of my lover,
but soon, go my own way.
Daisies and lovers are much the same—and love is best
when it's not contained.

## HAIKU #36

I harvested poetry—
as fiddleheads—by a stone
wall in the forest.


## HAIKU #37

I walked streets where
children play—thinking thoughts
I will not write.


## HAIKU #38

I listen and
forget about the white hat.

# HAD I NOT FOUND LOVE

Hands do not need to be washed,
before lovers embrace.
I know this because,
I've seen romance blossom
into friendship, and then into trust.
I've held my lover after a day's work
enough times to say;
I have no idea
who I might have been,
if she and I did not fall in love this way.

# LETTER TO THE FUTURE

Dear Future,

Nothing makes sense!

Ours is a society oppressed by prosperity. The people's clamoring for the betterment of a governed society has only encouraged our despotic know-it-alls to rape our planet. The working people's tolerance has come in but one form—silence. Silence has been the greatest of all injustices which I've witnessed, and the surest way out of our revolution.

I hope when you read this letter there has been a homeless president... just once! I hope the people have finally sided with other people—their brothers and sisters in the human race—over policy or tax breaks—over their comforts or disposition.

Our people's system of government has failed for centuries to serve the best interests of the people who have most deserved fairness and justice.

Did I not make that clear?

Our system has never put the best interests of the people first. Men and women have not realized that we, *ourselves*, must put our common interests first without the oversight of the oligarchy. If we do a new definition of leader could emerge. This new definition of leader would be one independent of control, and selfishness, and austerity.

But the people's convictions have continued to rest in how governments regulate society. In turn, our politicians have kept their interests within governance.

If you are witness to a people's day it was because men and women realized the worth which we have as humankind. It was because the supposed, and tenuous, worth based on an economic structure avowed to productivity and superiority was rejected. It was because cooperation and liberty prevailed over greed and degradation.

Coercion has been the greatest enemy to compassion and equality which people have faced in my lifetime! People are kept away from the grave injustices which are prevalent in society, simply, to ward off the potential for revolution.

I honestly believe you will read this and appreciate the sacrifices that so many people made, over so many centuries, which have resulted in the freedoms people in your time enjoy. Please use your knowledge, of these sacrifices, as a contributing force for your own conviction, that you too can set a course which will promote a better world for your future!

Peace!

# OTHERWISE WE ARE DUST

Long before I ever loved you,
there was a star.
And this most distant
and purest white star,
ceased,
 just before you were born.
All things natural
are but one,
but do also transform.
I believe we have in our hearts
the souls of dead stars.
 Your heart—your soul—your beauty
—and fire—
all are as bright and as pure
as that one distant star
which is, otherwise, dust.

# ONE DAY

Inspired by 'Let Us' by Alan Kaufman

May I listen to my heart
and hear silence.
May I empty my soul
in the pursuit of peace.
Earth is wrought
with wars and solemn prayers.
But its very essence, speaks
of the stillness of my faith.
It is your stillness, too.
May we then be vagrants;
may we fall from grace;
may we, that much more,
oppose evil. Our prayers
could speak truth,
and violence cease.

## ALL THAT I WILL

I am a poet. Life exists as I see it
so that I may create.
I am the god of my own universe;
and the stars,
which guide the currents of this universe,
are but tools
which I use to write poetry.
But I cannot pretend,
that being god has granted me omniscience.
This universe, which has multitudes
and anomalies,
that serve only to inspire,
exists beyond what I can fathom.
I am an obtuse god/poet.
All I that I will,
serves only that I know how to live.

## HAIKU #39

I am light seeking
shadows—in them I burn
still brighter.

## HAIKU #40

Taste life's sweetness;
but find wisdom in sacrifice.

## HAIKU #41

Far beyond the eye,
and deep within my living
soul, rests with the heart—

# STANDING UP IN THE SKY OF WINTER

Yesterday, I lifted my head
as if the sunrise was a call made directly to me.
I heard the winds against the side of my home,
ever so soft. They spoke
as if I were to brave wintery colds
with the desire to make myself stronger—hardier
—and sturdier—
each time I set foot into this world.

But today it is not winter.
I can scarcely hear a sound from beyond the walls of my home.
And I'm not inclined
to venture any further than to my window frame.
It is not that the outside is not welcoming enough—nor too hostile.
But I am maybe too simple;
I do not answer to the desire within me;
the desire which calls that I set myself free. I stay put.
I become entrenched
in the commonsense of the everyday which I so long had not.

Tomorrow will be another day,
but my fortunes will not turn
until I stop feeling that good
will serve to quell my thirst for the uncompromising.
I need winter back.
It will inspire me.

I need to have a day where the sky comes falling down to let me wear a
long, brilliant white coat, which I will hold proudly on my shoulders.

# OF DREAMS AND LEAVES

Sitting, under a sugar maple,
lower extremities—feet and ankles—to my hips.
I embrace this forested earth
covered by autumn leaves; and dream of an
escape to other worlds.

My body, it is earth bound,
almost as a seed.
But my mind reaches off into the heavens;
dreams are cast off as autumn leaves.

# ROAD TRIP

With nothing but a penchant for adventure, I left.
I left that I could rediscover places
Which, once, I was passing through, blindly,
as I winded my way through madness. Years ago,
I stopped in a town
to unfetter my soul
from the constraints of being misunderstood.  Yesterday,
I RETurned to this town, and
I've learned from these trips to now familiar places
that freedom is not normal.

# ALL THAT IS WILL EVER BE

I sit here, basking shirtless in the sunshine, and I feel the hard jagged surface of rock under the soles of my work boots. I wonder and listen. All that I have within my mind is forgotten for brief instances, as I unravel, in each and the next moment.

Books I've read, and been present with, have held their place; but more often, I think of people—and unplanned adventures—and think of what I am.

I am the long forgotten words of teachers, and friends. I am my family. I am this mountaintop where I sit, trying to be present, with all that is around me. I have filled my soul with the songs of these birds, cool air, and beautiful sunshine.

# THIRSTY

Grey skies hide in the corner of my eye,
I am thirsty.
Hunched forward
to duck branches of trees,
I peer through the forest, and
almost see the horizon.
Out beyond the pines and their shadows,
further up the slope of the mountain, is a magical lake.
I've been there before.
I've seen my reflection in its waters.
I've witnessed this reflection vanish
—and at once, my dreams took to the sky—
but fell back to earth. One day
a dream will take flight,
it will become a god's dream,
and entire worlds
will be constructed
so that it may have life. I am thirsty.

## HAIKU # 42
Lost souls;
please, will you nourish our
next incarnation

## HAIKU #43
I dreamed that
the sky was the womb
of all things.

## HAIKU #44
I am the illusion
that lights the path to godliness.

## NOT A COFFEE POEM

Empty and
sitting on my table;
a coffee mug
in pieces. I
fill it with tears.

# TO TEACH

what teachers have taught me
in school, I learned how to write
how to formulate equations
teachers taught that I could go places
and see the world
see the world through a lens of astonishment

in school I learned
I learned from different sorts of teachers
some taught me that I needed discipline
now, as an adult
I'm studious, disciplined and outgoing
others taught me to hold nothing back

teachers inspire generations
they also
lead many down paths which, at best
only allow them to follow directions
teachers cannot, alone, change the world
our teachers need us to change first

young people learn so much
they learn all that is not spoken in class
teachers have taught me many lessons,
which words do not capture
try as they might—
much of what I've learned was despite my teachers

teachers have taught me
how to find, in this world a learning path
one where my dreams
transform themselves into purpose
our teachers cannot fulfill this need for change
without, first, us giving teachers inspiration

my teachers taught me that I can inspire
I was once the inspiration
with which my teachers to lead *me* to success
and now, I too, must be a teacher
because I'm so inspired by what the future holds
what might I, now, teach

# A DAISY

Here I am, a daisy,
grasses are by my side.
What I have
I give to the bees and the winds—
hoping with them
love may reside.

Bees imbibe nectar,
ripe from springtime rains.
Away they go after a sip,
as if winds spoke a lover's name.

And in the winds too
may my dreams and pollen go.

## BLESSED BE THE TRUTH

Truth has not one form; it is not rigid like block or brick or stone. And if you reached out to grasp truth it would separate from its own image. You would open your hand and see only empty space as truth quickly flew off, and away. Truth is something that seekers of knowledge and lovers of art know to be too discreet for others eyes. Yes! Truth is in all things close to your heart if you find in yourself that truth is dear. Protect her and bless us all with your compassion, honesty, and tender spirit – be yourself a guardian of the truth.

# WHY AM I NOT MORE SURPRISED

All my life you've eluded me.
Yet, here I stay, where I once was lost.
Because only here
can I rightfully say I've not given up.
You are out there
—somewhere—waiting—
and I will find you.
Each time I venture out, searching,
I become stronger;
I become more hopeful.
Hills become less daunting,
and valleys less treacherous.
Only one thing
keeps us apart.  It is a secret.
And a secret which at once,
I cannot keep to myself,
and cannot express in words.

## STARS AS DANCERS

Stars as dancers,
under moonlit sky,
hang as if held up
by my imagination.
A ballet.
A ballet.

# ACKNOWLEDGEMENTS

I have very little in the way of a formal education; but from having had mentors, who helped me to move faster towards acquiring the skills and knowledge I needed to write well, I have been fortunate in the most profound way. I've turned my life around in the process of becoming a writer. Also, thankfully, I've been fortunate to have had a few of the poems in this book published in online magazines and in journals. Because of the successes I've had in this process of becoming a poet and essayist and mad pride activist—I'd like to give special thanks to my mother and father for their loving support. I'd like to thank Charles Monette and Vince Cioffi for their guidance which has helped me to blossom as an artist. And I'd like to give mention to Tomorrow's Builders, Vermont Views, Counterpoint, Sling Shot, The Mindful Word, Open Minds Quarterly, Cannon's Mouth and Parallax for publishing my essays and poetry.

www.ingramcontent.com/pod-product-compliance
Lightning Source LLC
Chambersburg PA
CBHW030154070426

42447CB00032B/1187